FARM

FARM

Paintings, drawings and Somerset voices

Kate Lynch

by **KATE LYNCH**

First published in 2017 by Furlong Fields Publishing
Illustrations © Kate Lynch 2017
www.katelynch.co.uk

ISBN 978 09544394 6 0

Words recorded and edited by Kate Lynch
Design and layout © Lyn Davies Design
Printed and bound in England by Hamptons, Bristol
Photography of artwork by Delmar Studio, Taunton

cover   Carl with the blower, Over Stratton orchards (Burrow Hill Cider)

half title   Cider apples for pressing

frontispiece   Baling grass for silage, Butleigh Road Farm

this page   Broadcasting grass seed with the fiddle

back cover   Jeff Cracknell and the Christmas geese

Contents

Foreword

Kate Lynch is an artist and writer whose achievements already include some memorable books exploring aspects of Somerset's rural life. In this new collection her focus widens as she captures the voices and experience of a group of Somerset farmers, and their families, who have lived through times of unprecedented change.

Their farms lie mostly in central Somerset, south of the Mendip Hills, a landscape as rich and varied as any in the South West of England. Some who tell their stories here are relative newcomers to farming. Many have farming roots that reach back through the generations. All are remarkable for their resilience and adaptability as they continue to face the economic and practical transformations farming has undergone since the Second World War. They are notable too for an understandable pride in what they do. Farming isn't a job, they insist, it's a way of life.

The book is important not least because it preserves the memories of its older contributors. They are now among the last witnesses to a lost world of farming which endured for centuries and which still helps to define our sense of Somerset. It was a world of small mixed farms, where a dozen milking cows, with some sheep, pigs and

bringing the cows home

poultry, and crops to feed them, were enough to provide a decent living, where cheese was made plentifully in this rich cheese country, and where in almost every village the cider presses worked through the autumn days.

Somerset farmers, as this book makes clear, now seek

to build on what has always been locally distinctive. Their farms and herds may often be larger, but dairying and stock rearing still have a key part to play, specialist cider and cheese making flourish, willows are grown for the basketmaker, and the fields continue to be ploughed and sown to meet the needs of the modern world.

Kate Lynch's beautifully illustrated book is vivid in its human detail. It is also an important record of how, within the span of living memory, Somerset farming has changed fundamentally.

TOM MAYBERRY
South West Heritage Trust

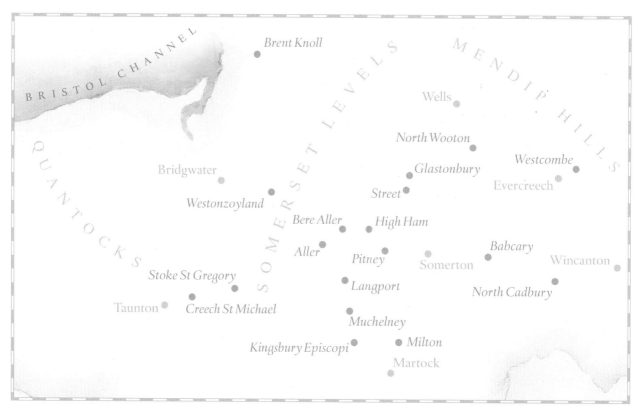

● *Featured farms*   ● Nearby towns

The Saddleback sow and piglets, Glebe Farm

Butterwell Farm *Pitney*

Pete Cox

My grandparents were Emelyn and James, they lived here and had their children here, then my father farmed with my grandfather. There were pigs, the sows would be one side and the little piglets on the other, and the piglets could go through. There were 14 cows, they were tie-ups in the milking parlour, that's when they lie in two's – there's part of the building still there. They'd have their kale and mangles and hay they'd feed them on. Father expanded a little bit and got to 18 cows. They had chickens and they made hay and their own straw. My grandparents made cheese and there was a stamp, but my father never did. Out on the road here there was a well, it's covered over now, it's on the side of the road, on the verge in the corner of the orchard. They used to keep their cheese in it, to keep it cool, before fridges. That's why this is called Butterwell Farm. My grandfather also had a cider press, he used to make cider, probably for his own consumption and various other people around. All the farms would have been much the same in that era.

Obviously when my father was young he milked by hand. I never milked by hand, we already had the machine with the bucket at the top, then you take the bucket and tip it into the churn. Father always brought the cows back to milk them here because the land was quite close to the farm. I always helped out and when I left school at 15 I worked full time on the farm. I drove tractors from when I was about 11 or 12 year old. When I was young I used to get paid two shillings and sixpence for mucking out the cows every weekend. I always wanted to work on the farm, for as long as I can remember. I lived here until I was 22, then moved down the road when I married. I came back here in 1988. There were lots of farms in my time. There was Cullens at Chapel Farm just up the road, that was ongoing, and Alan Hill at Lortie, and Greystones, and Hawkins, a state farm. There was Mike Cox, myself, Ron Cox, Meakers and Dave Oram. That's just in this village. There were about eight milking. Everyone had a similar number of cows, somewhere around 16 or 18 cows, that was a living. Milk was a better price then.

Milking time, Butterwell Farm

Pete Cox

I've been milking cows for nearly half a century, it's not so bad as you think – if you want to go somewhere you milk early. We're milking at half past six, seven o'clock, and then again at half past five in the afternoon, so you finish by ten in the morning and around eight o'clock at night.

A cow's about two and a half years old when she has her first calf. When they calf for the first time and you start milking them they can kick a bit, they might dance a bit, people have been killed in milking parlours. I've been kicked unconscious in the stalls years ago, I went backwards against the wall. Animals do tend to be quieter now, perhaps it's the breeding. There was a really good Friesian bull in my time, it was called Howard Emperor the 25th. Of course we didn't know the bull, it was artificial insemination, we just asked for that particular semen, lots of farmers did. This bull threw really good calves, they were really good milk producers, but they were a devil to break in, we had major problems milking them, but they gave loads of milk. We breed from our quietest cows, but if you're nervous a cow can pick it up. You have to be wary but confident, especially when you're my height, that's when it is better to be six feet tall, you can put your shoulder into them more easily.

For small farms in the early 1990s, when they brought in milk quotas, things got quite hard then. It wasn't enough to be milking a couple of dozen cows and I started to do other work as well, like fencing and hedge trimming. I still do it now. Our cows have always been outside through the summer, from April. It's their nature to be outside, they eat grass. You should see them when it's time to put them out after the winter, they will be hanging around the door of the barn when it's sunny, they know when it's time – they love the sun, and when they are out in the fields again they're running around, dancing, kicking, tails in the air. You can feel they are happy. We know all our cows, they've all got names. We've got a herd of about 100 with the calves and heifers and we're milking 32 – mainly Friesians and some Dairy Shorthorns and Jerseys.

If I had been going to stay in milking, we might have gone into Jerseys. We've not got a great acreage of land, and I'm looking to the future now that I'm getting older. I'm going to give up the milking and go into rearing calves. 32 milking cows isn't viable now. The price for a standard litre is 20.9 pence, ours is a little better mostly because our butterfat's quite good because of the Jerseys. The price varies, but we were at about 32–33 pence two years ago. We're going to keep two of the Jerseys, our favourites, even when we give up milking, it's nostalgic, but we won't milk them.

Pete milking, Butterwell Farm

Butleigh Road Farm *Glastonbury*

Les Davies

I was born in 1937. Our garden used to come out at the bottom of Mr Reed's farm , Cranhill Road, Street. I used to ride the horse down to fetch the cows when I was seven or eight. I went on and worked for him when I left school, I was 15. He paid me three pounds and sixpence a week. He had about 30 cows at that time, that were quite big in they day I suppose. He had a milk round. He had people work for him, he had cowmen lived in the houses, this would be the beginning of the 1950s. It was seven days a week. I started about six in the morning and you used to milk at night and finished up at six or seven in the evening, well, longer if you were haymaking. I used to enjoy it, I still do now.

We used to hunt the cows all down there into the fields and back again for milking, that's what we used to do years ago, of course all that's gone, it's completely different today. We used to tie them up in a cow stall and milk them sitting on a three-legged stool and we milked by hand in the fields – you wouldn't be allowed to do it now with the hygiene and so on. We used to cool the churns in the ditch, kept the milk cool. There were farms everywhere, mostly milking, lots of small dairy farmers. Everybody had 30 or 40 cows round here in they days. I suppose the biggest farm round here then was Tibbs',

he used to milk nearly 100 cows, big farm up on the hill there, that's all gone, that finished years ago. There were so many farms milking, there were I, Dave Sandford, Matt King, Johnny Lock, Vic King, Bill, Tom King, Colin Stacey, Bakers over Street, Jim Birds, Tinney … that's more than ten of them – and Reg Percy. That was just round in this area, about two miles either way. I could keep rattling them on, like Dave Cullen, he used to milk, and Jim Masters, he sold up a couple of year ago. They go and there's no one to take their place, smaller ones get out, that's the trouble.

I remember when I were at school I had to go out of school to the dairy with the trolley. I used to get picked to go and fetch the milk – I used to go out Westend in Street, get the trolley, load it up with milk, they were the bottles, a third of a pint. I were 13 or 14 I suppose. I used to take the crates round the classrooms, then when they'd finished I collected them and I'd take them back. I used to love it because I used to get out of all the lessons. I absolutely hated school, I couldn't wait to leave. I couldn't get out quick enough, I just wanted to milk cows and drive tractors, that's all I wanted to do. And I've been doing it ever since. I haven't regretted it, not one bit. The main thing is if you've got the work and you're happy doing it.

Les and Colin in the yard, Butleigh Road Farm

Thomas in the barn, Butleigh Road Farm

Les Davies

What happened with the farm was that Clarks wanted to buy Mr Reed's land so he sold it and moved up here. Then in 1961 we took it on. We rent most of the land and own some. When we took over we had 40 cows. Now we've got 120 cows and 100 followers – about 220 calves and heifers in calf. We are milking 120 and about 100 are replacements. We rear all our cows. We're farming 300 acres, you need all that to be organic – for every one acre you need for conventional farming you need two acres if you are organic. We were lucky because Colin always wanted to do farming. If he hadn't wanted to do it I would have got out of it years ago because I couldn't have done it on my own at my age. Now Colin's son, Thomas, works for us and Colin's step-grandson, he's coming on, he's doing an apprenticeship in farming. We're four generations now. We start about six, then we finish about half six, seven o'clock at night – it's about six hours a day milking and cleaning up. Then there's all the other work to do – silage and hay, the vets, et cetera, and we do the ditches from October onwards until the birds start nesting.

The cows are all in house for the winter, middle of October till April they're in, but the rest of the time they're out, out in the far fields during the day, and in fields closer to home at night. They stroll back in and stroll back out, it's not a stressful life. Some are kept in all the time nowadays – you don't see too many dairy cows out in the fields now, they are getting few and far between.

Thomas Davies

Farming's not a job, it's a way of life, the cows have got to be fed, they've got to be looked after as well as a human, you're like any carer. When you come down here and you've got a cow on calving, if she's struggling you go in, you're helping her. I've calved hundreds of cows in the twelve years I've worked here and you get the biggest satisfaction because you've saved the cow and you've brought new life in. Since I was seven I was always out here with Grandad and Dad and when I left school I knew I was going to be down here. When I started, if I was milking 80 cows I was milking a lot, whereas now we've reached 120 this year, that's the most we've ever got up to. I enjoy milking because you're in here with the cows and you've got that connection with them. Each cow, every one of them, is different, I know every one of them as they walk in. I can identify every one of them just by looking at their bags.

Thomas Davies

I'm glad it's more modern than it was because I've heard Grandad tell stories of when they used to unload twelve hundred small bales of hay a day between three of them – load them up and unload them. And I know Granny's said that when she used to help them they'd be chucking the hay off the trailers, and the snakes would be coming off the trailers that had got into the hay, there would be snakes sliding off the side of trailers all the time they were unloading, and she didn't do it after that, she couldn't put up with that. And when Grandad used to go milking with the milking bails, it used to take him longer to milk 30 or 40 cows than what it takes me now to milk 120. It's easier now really.

I know it's still long hours and there is a lot of hard work involved, but it's easier work to do – you've got the modern kit, the air conditioning that makes it bearable in the summer, because up until two years ago I never had air conditioning on my tractor. Once I'm on the tractor time flies, it's heaven, I love it on there. Up in there now you've got your radio on, you've got your air conditioning, you've got a different view with every journey you do.

We make all our own silage for the cows' winter feed. We done our first cut this year in eight days, that was 1,475 bales. I was down here some nights till half past eleven, so long as the lights were working on the trailer I'd keep going. When I started here that would have taken us about three weeks, because they had the individual wrapper. Grandad used to cut it, Dad would haul it up in the afternoon and bale it the following day, and Grandad would wrap it. We've halved it because, with the wrapper behind the tractor, and the baler, Dad's doing the job of two men in one go now. I struggle to keep up with hauling it.

I love working on the farm. If I go into a field and it's full up with thistles and stinging nettles and I've topped it and it's nice and tidy and not a weed standing, I've had a good day. If I've emptied a field of silage I've had a good day. So long as I've got something to show for it at the end of the day I'm happy.

Glebe Farm *Pitney*

David Walrond

There was never any electric up at Glebe Farm and no mains water. My uncle could have had electricity but when the electricity came to Pitney he said, 'Why would I want electricity?' Water was from the well, there was a pump with a long rocker arm. For the house they mostly used one bucket a day, more on washdays. There was another well and another pump outside for the animals. In the dry times there was a lot of carrying of water, and I remember people carrying water with yokes. Uncle Perce had eight cows and sheep and a couple of pigs. The pigs were mainly for the house. He had chickens too. In those days there were lots of small farms, it was a way of life. You didn't buy something until you had the money to pay for it. The farms were mostly passed down in families and there were a few tenanted farms. Everyone had a few cows, there were at least ten small farms milking in Pitney. They were all through the village. We all hand-milked. I started when I was about nine years old, sometimes I milked before school – and weekends. As a child we all did jobs, helped with haymaking, led the horse when they were picking up hay, you were always shutting the gate and taking the cows to different fields.

A chap used to come down from Somerton, he used to come down on his bike and he'd kill the pig one day, hang it up, split it, then come down the next day and cut it up, and for that he used to charge twelve shillings in the 1950s.

We used to kill two a year, one November time, the other February time. During the war we were allowed to kill two a year for your own use. We used to have a back kitchen, no windows, all dark, and there were big stretchers. My mother used to salt the meat, she had great pots of salt and she just kept rubbing it in, she used to do it for two or three days, same with the bacon, that was cured, hung up. It was all fat bacon in those days, I was brought up on that – you'd have a slice in the frying pan in the morning and have enough fat to cook your eggs, fried potato and fried bread. It was pure fat, you just cooked it until it all scrumped up.

My uncle used to have a bull and I remember when I was very young, when we had a cow in season I used to help hunt it up here, but once we had the cow in the yard I had to come indoors while the bull was serving the cow – but then when I got to a certain age I was suddenly allowed to stay outside! I left school when I was 14 to help farm with my father and uncle.

Hazel and I came up here to Glebe in the 1980s after my last aunt died. There was still no mains water or electricity and there was only an outdoor earth closet, so we had a lot to do. Our children grew up here. Rob was always interested in farming. I remember the first time he did the milking, he was 14 or 15, and Hazel and I went off for a day and we didn't have to come back at four o'clock for milking, it was wonderful.

Rob feeding the sow and piglets, Glebe Farm

Rob Walrond

I was born in 1963. When I was a boy I helped take the cows out to the fields. It's hard to believe now that 14 cows provided a living for a family. We would let them out from the yard and I'd walk with them down the road to Low Ham, past the playing field, with nobody in front of them, and, as they got to the field, I would walk on through them and open the gate so they could go on into the field. Or I'd take them the other way. I'd do that before school in the mornings and then I'd sometimes help Dad finish off the milking and take the cows back out in the evening. Uncle Percy farmed about 70 acres up here and Dad farmed about 30 acres at Hillside. Hillside was rented and Dad and Uncle Percy farmed Hillside and Glebe in partnership – a few milking cows, a few beef cattle, sheep, a couple of pigs, a bit of corn. Mum and Dad moved up to Glebe after my aunt died, about the time I was just going off to university to do agriculture. I knew the farm wasn't big enough to sustain an income for another family, so my idea was to get a job in farm management. It's what I did until the farmer who owned the farm sold up, so then I looked for another job closer to Pitney – the draw of the home farm was strong, and I wanted to help Dad out a bit more. Then for about 14 years I had a full-time job and helped out on the farm here as well.

We started selling direct in the late 1990s – meat and sausages – and Liz was keen on growing vegetables, so we extended the garden and Liz had a little trailer on the back of her bike and delivered boxes of vegetables round the village. We gradually got more confident and decided to convert to organic – we'd gone down the intensive route but we didn't feel happy pushing the land and the animals too hard, so organic farming seemed a lot more in line with our views.

With organic rules you have to be what's called 'extensive' with the sheep, so you don't keep them in the same field for a long time. We rent grass keep down on the moor at Coombe about three miles away and I've put some of the ewes down there with their lambs, it's been dry and we wouldn't normally be able to put them down there at this time of year. They're coming back Wednesday night for dagging when we tidy up their bottoms. We've never been blessed with good sheepdogs, but we are blessed with plenty of relatives, so we get lots of people involved. We try to do it on a Sunday afternoon or an evening when there's less traffic because we have to go on the main road for a short stretch. With 113 ewes and lambs, it's quite an occasion. Then, after that, shearing will be in just over a month, end of May.

Running the flock from the moor up to Glebe Farm

The hen house, Glebe Farm

Rob Walrond

There were always cattle here – there still are – and pigs, sheep and hens. My grandmother used to keep 40 or 50 chickens. We've got 600 laying hens and you really notice how much they like grazing, scratching around for worms, they nearly all come out most times of the year. The hardest thing about keeping chickens is in mid-summer when you've got to stay up until about half past ten to shut them in at night. We don't take any chances, even with an electric fence. Late spring, early summer, when the vixens are feeding the cubs, that's when we've had problems in the past.

We got pigs about the time we went organic. I'd never kept pigs and Dad hadn't kept pigs since his youth, when they had one or two pigs in the sty and farmyard and they'd be let out into the woodland in the summer. We can't let them into the woodland like they used to, but all our pigs are outside. We always make a wet wallow for them when it's dry and hot. One of the things that's lovely about having outdoor pigs is they can follow their natural behaviour, they can root the ground up. It's a bit hard at the moment, but as soon as we get some rain again they'll be turning the ground over, ploughing it up, they literally spend hours rooting round, which is great to see. When you come to feed them, as soon as the Landrover drives into the field they are racing around with excitement, and they really get to use their legs and their muscles. They're so active. They have such strong muscles in their noses, that's what they're built for, digging up roots, turning the stones over, eating the grubs, that's what they love.

It's a four year rotation. When these leave we'll sow spring barley. The goodness in the soil comes from the pigs, then the corn is milled and fed to the next generation. It's cyclical, one generation provides the fertility for the next. Almost half their feed is what we've produced on the farm here. It's not a million miles away from what Grandfather would have done in his time, apart from so much is mechanised now.

We can never compete on scale and on producing the cheapest commodity possible, but we get a lot of pleasure from meeting people in our shop and sharing what we're doing. All the family help out when they can – our three daughters all have an interest in helping things go well on the farm, which is great.

Cracknell's Farm *Langport*

Tony Cracknell

I left school at 14, the war was still on, and Father said, 'You come home and work for me and I'll give you half a crown a week and a shilling of that you give back to your mother to keep you'. So that was my starting wage. There were no grumbles, I was alright, I had all I wanted. I was milking goats first, then we got cows. When you start milking by hand properly the muscles in your arm just screw up and refuse to work, but I'd been milking goats so I was used to it. We had to get the milk on the road by eight o'clock in the morning, take the churn to the farm gate. You did as you were told in those days! A farmer over the hill, he had a herd of cows, quite a sizeable farm, and there were five or six of us hand-milking at his farm – I had to go over there as well, afternoon milking, get the cows in, tie them up, and take a stool and sit underneath them. I got something extra for that, not much, because the farming wages weren't much. When we got married some years later, farming wages were still only about seven pounds a week.

We came straight down here when we married in 1954, right after our honeymoon. We bought it at auction – four acres with a little bungalow and a corrugated shed which had blown down. We propped it up and Mr Higgins he made the field into hay for me that first year and put it in the shed and that kept the shed standing with the hay! I worked for Commander Prideaux for a month milking. Then I got a job with Mr Body and then with Mr Higgins – they both had chickens. I was thinking of going into calves, but then I got chickens of my own – twelve cockerels to start with and a hen to keep them warm, that was the first chickens we had. I used to go round in a van and knock on doors and say, 'How about having a chicken this weekend?', and I sold firewood too, and eggs. Chicken was more special then, a chicken would last a family three days. We couldn't afford to go into battery production, we were at the beginning of free range because we couldn't afford to do otherwise. We bought more fields and gradually we built up. We've got 46 acres now. We keep sheep too. We started off with goats, we milked them, and then we got some lambs. We don't have goats any more, but we still keep sheep. We had geese in the early days, the gander used to run after my wife. So it's all gone on from there. We still have geese for Christmas. And we have nearly 2,000 chickens. All the birds are free range and our son Jeff and his family run the farm now.

Sunnyside Farm *North Wootton*

James Bartlett

Our parents always had animals on the farm and that's what inspired us to want to go farming. Initially they hand-reared a few calves and then they got a herd of pedigree North Devons. My brother and I specialise in sheep now. They're Friesland mostly but some of them are Dorset-crossed. We keep the lambs on the ewes for about six weeks. We're organic and that means all the milk fed to the lambs must be from the ewes. We keep all the ewe lambs and a local farmer takes the ram lambs. We've got lambing sheds just near the parlour so we can lamb indoors. It keeps them out of the weather and it stops the foxes getting the lambs. Foxes will take lambs. Frieslands are good at lambing – they're slim sheep but big and roomy, and they look after their lambs well. From that point of view there are not too many problems. The milking is quite straightforward – it's much like a cow parlour, just on a smaller scale. The sheep come up onto a platform to be milked. There's room for twelve sheep on the platform and we milk six while we're washing the others. They're quite well-behaved. They twitch a little for the first couple of weeks when they're young and then they settle down. They get fed in the parlour so they love coming in and queue up outside and bash on the door to be let in.

When we started, we milked for about the first three years and just sold milk. It wasn't really a very profitable way of going about things. Then we were extremely lucky. A lady called Mary Holbrook, a very respected cheese-maker, was going to sell her sheep flock and agreed to give us a lesson and show us how her cheese was made. We bought her recipe and the cheese moulds from her. The cheese was called Little Ryding, named after one of her fields. So, we have her to thank for all that. We now make nine different cheeses, but the Little Ryding always has a special place for us and it's popular. We also make yoghurt from the sheep milk. It's lovely – thick, creamy and slightly sharp – a traditional old-fashioned yoghurt. We also make cheese from our cows' milk. We used to keep pigs and piglets and all the whey used to go to them, they loved it. The ground is quite good, but there is heavy clay in places, so it can get pretty waterlogged at times – keeping pigs was a bit of a messy business. We hope to keep some again in the future though.

The farm is about 200 acres, about half of that is rented and it's not as big as it sounds. It was always cheese country round here and there are still several farms making cheese traditionally.

School Farm *Muchelney*

Graham Walker

My great-grandparents came here as tenant farmers in the 1890s. My great-granddad bred draught horses, broke them in and sold them for pulling carts in towns. Then later they started milking. They had the chance to buy the farm in the 1920s. What made a big difference was the railway coming. There was hardly any milking here before the railway came, then in 1930 Nestle's built the factory down at Thorney, so you had a ready outlet for milk then. I know Grandfather milked up to 14 cows by hand. You could make a living milking a dozen or so cows then. Seems incredible now.

I never had a milking herd. All the red cows are Red Devon breeding cows. The others are crossed with an Angus bull. They're all in calf at the moment. This time of year I come out on the moor to check the cattle every day, the biggest hazard is if you get one fall in the ditch. They come in for the winter mainly because of the damage they'd do to the ground, it would just turn into a quagmire. Where they come from, North Devon, some places up there they've got hard land on hills with rock underneath. They can keep them out all winter there, they're quite happy so long as they've got food and water, but they do need somewhere dry to lie down. If they're out on our land they just turn it into the Somme within a matter of a few weeks if it's wet. It floods here – you can feel the ground moving, because it's just a big sponge. In 2014, when there was a lot of water and we were an island for nine weeks, where we're stood now, the water level would have been about a foot over our heads. My cousin, he farms at Muchelney Ham, he's 77, and he reckons it was about a foot deeper than anything he'd ever seen. It's not unprecedented though because my grandfather knew one like it in the 1920s, which is out of living memory now, but he showed me where the high tide line was then. Our house is nice and dry, but the land can flood. When you do get the flood it rises steadily, so if you have got animals down here and you see the river overflowing, you've got a day to do something about it. It's an unusual place to farm I suppose. Underneath there's a layer of peaty material, very coarse, and I know, when I've dug a gatepost hole, you go through a clay material for eight to ten inches and then you've got this fibrous material and the remains of rushes in there. Sometimes you find a piece of bog oak, it's about three or four thousand years old, it's so soft you can put a spade through it, but it's still very recognisable as a piece of wood. It was a swamp going back in time – it was the monks at the Abbey who were the first ones to start draining it properly, until we get to where we are now.

Graham on the moor, November

Graham scraping the yard, January

Graham Walker

I was born in 1960. I can remember the last horse Grandad still used to come down here every day with the cart to go milking. As I got older me and Grandad worked quite well together. Then when I took on the farm in the 1980s, I started market gardening. It was the one thing you could start with a wheelbarrow and a bag of seeds without a huge capital investment, and that did quite well for a number of years. I remember when a beautiful white cauliflower was about a pound in money at the farm shop and a gallon of petrol was 84 pence – well, the same cauliflower now is about 60 pence in the supermarket and a gallon of petrol is at least five pounds! The money's not there in vegetables any more. We're very small, one of the smallest about, we have about 50 acres and rent a bit more. We've got the farm shop and we sell Helen's pies and our meat and sausages, and some other local produce, and we do cream teas in the summer – it all helps. We rear cattle and a few sheep and pigs. The pigs are Oxford Sandy and Blacks – we buy weaners and raise them. I don't want to keep pigs through the winter, it's so muddy, and if you're going to have breeding sows you really need to house them in the winter.

They're a traditional breed and they do very well – not too much fat, but enough fat to make them cook nicely.

The cows come in December-time for the winter. We scrape up two to three times a week – obviously the concrete's got to be a bit damp otherwise you just can't scrape up, it just sticks there, and you can't do it when it's frosty either. It's a 1958 Massey Ferguson FE35 tractor. We like our old machines, I do all the repairs. I just keep scraping until the muck spreader's full. Luckily we're not in a nitrate-free zone or we wouldn't be able to spread the muck in the winter.

The winter is where most of the work is really. In the summer you're making hay and silage, but when the cows are in there's something to do every day – feeding them, scraping up and they've got to have fresh straw put down.

This lot of cows are all in calf, but this is the last lot. They will raise the calves then that will be it after that, I shall sell the cows and just buy calves in then. Our son will probably do something else, he's more interested in sheep than cattle and I can't say I blame him – if you get knocked over by a sheep it hurts less than if you get knocked over by a cow!

Overton Farm *Babcary*

Ken Paull

I remember when Hazlegrove School started up, we supplied them with milk in a churn, and then in the 1950s regulations came in and it had to be pasteurised and bottled. I remember taking the churn up to the school each morning and dropping it off and when it went to bottles they moaned because it was so much easier to dip it out of the churn! We had about 50 cows up at Camel Hill, that was quite big then, and we had about 20 to 30 ewes, I can remember shearing them, and Mother had chickens, she had chickens in folding units. I used to push a wheelbarrow out there with the feed and collect the eggs, change the straw, and this sort of thing. She used to sell eggs to the egg packing station down Sparkford, they used to come round and collect the eggs every week. We had pigs too. We used to have a pig that was killed during the War, I can remember the pig killing. I remember Mother and Father rubbing salt into the hams in the kitchen after the pig was killed. We reared piglets as well. In the 1960s, when Father died, that's when we gave up the other animals and just had the cows.

We had a small milk round for several years – but milk rounds were diminishing, so then we started going to farmers' markets, selling milk and cream. We went up to Notting Hill with a neighbour and he was selling his meat, December time. The first time we went up there I can remember one lady coming up and saying, 'Oh this takes me back, I can remember when my mother had a cow in the back garden', which they did during the War, they had cows and chickens in back gardens.

David and Rose run the farm now, they make yoghurt and sell the milk and cream, it's all unpasteurised. The cows are all Guernseys, always were. It's full cream milk like the old days – thick, deep and creamy on the top. There were lots of farms when I was growing up. Everyone had milk churns. I remember one chap, he used to take his churn in an old wheelbarrow every day to the milk factory at Sparkford, it was a mile or so down a lane. He only had a couple of cows. There were over 20 farms or smallholdings in this village, Babcary. They had between four and ten cows each – they had a pig, a few hens and milked a few cows and grew their feed. They were all small mixed farms. There are three working farms in the village today. The ones that are left have got bigger.

Southend Farm *High Ham*

Luke Timewell

I was born in 1992. My grandfather was Cuthbert Stokes. He was a general farm worker at Vigar Webb's place, Henley Farm. I was down there when I was seven or eight – every weekend, every school holiday. I lived it, breathed it. It's houses now, but back then it was a busy farm. In the early 1900s they made cheese there, but when I knew it they just milked cows. I used to open up gates, let the cows through, shut gates, feed calves, bed up calves, then when I got a bit older I was allowed to scrape up the yard and drive tractors in the fields. I was about 12 when I drove tractors!

I worked for Richard Webb when I left school, milked cows, drove tractors. I hated school, I always knew what I wanted to do and I couldn't wait to get started. I always said I was going to have my own herd one day. I kept some sheep first, then I got my first cow – I bought a calf down the market, I was 18, I bought it for £16, I kept it for a few months and sold it for a profit. Then I bought five or six more and kept them down at Margaret Porter's.

Now me and Abbie have got our own milking unit. We've got British Friesians, Jerseys and a couple of Swedish Reds, that's a hardier breed and the quality of the milk's better. The Holstein Friesians give a lot of milk, but it's not got so much butterfat in it, you can see the colour's different. The Jerseys and the Swedish Reds give milk that's deeper in colour, creamier. We've also got a Shorthorn. We've been buying cows from Pete Cox, he's giving up. We're up to 32 cows now. We are renting this yard and about 80 acres. We make all our own silage and hay and still do a bit of contracting as well – it all helps.

The milking bail's an old one, we bought it off Mike Tucker. It's how they used to milk out on the moor. I expect if it could talk it would tell you its story. Most farms round here used milking bails on the moor in Grandad's day. Now this one's back in use in our yard – it's a dairy unit on a budget, but it works just fine. I think if the price of milk were better there could be more smaller units, which wouldn't be a bad thing.

We always check the cows at night. They're in for the winter now, and last night in that downpour I got absolutely drenched, it was about eleven o'clock and I've never known such a storm. Even when they're in the fields in the summer, last thing at night we drive round, shine the lights on them and check them, always, even if we get back late.

Luke and the milking bail, Southend Farm

Westcombe Dairy *Evercreech*

Richard Calver

My father came from a family of shoemakers in Norwich and made lasts for Winston Churchill's wife, Princess Margaret and Princess Elizabeth, so I didn't come from a farming family. I went into farming because my father took me on an old combine harvester when I was three, and I sat on the back and since then I always wanted to go farming. When I was at school I used to run up the hill and there used to be a man milking a cow by hand, I used to nip in when I was supposed to be doing something else! Then I used to cycle to a local farm to help clean out pigs when I was about eight or nine, this was near Northolt in London. When I left school I worked on farms. I learnt to milk cows in an old outside Hosier milking bail, I was there in the cold weather of 1962–3 and I remember there was a canvas roof and it split and all the snow came down on top of us while we were milking. Then I met a man in Somerset who had bought a farm and he was looking for a young chap to put in as a partner. I had the contents of my Austin A40 car, a dog and an armchair, and I slept in the kitchen with the dog at the beginning, and we gradually built it up. Twelve cows to start with.

There's a long tradition of cheesemaking round here, many of the farms had cheese rooms. There was a woman called Edith Cannon, a farmer's daughter, she used to make cheddar cheese here in the 1890s, and in 1897 she won the prize for the best cheese in the British Empire. Then she formed a cheese school in partnership with the Bath and West Society in Wells. My son Tom found her old recipe and we use the Cannon method in our cheesemaking. We've been developing our farmhouse cheddar since 1990 and Tom runs the cheesemaking now.

Cheddaring is the process of handling the curd. It's stacking the curd, that's cheddaring. It's to do with expanding the protein and forcing the whey out of the curd. So you cut the curd and turn it over and stack one on top of the other, it's the piling up of the slabs and the slabs, being quite heavy, push some extra whey out of the curd, which is what you want. That's what distinguishes the process, that's cheddaring. It's milled and salted after this and then put in moulds to mature. We don't have a horse and cart to take the cheese to market, but the cheddaring process is the old way it was always done, we do it by hand, we do it traditionally. We also make a ricotta cheese now and an Alpine-style cheese. It's all unpasteurised milk. We're milking 380 cows in two milking parlours. Our cows are outside most of the year, but they'll be coming in at the end of October for the winter.

Manor Farm *North Cadbury*

Jamie Montgomery

You can't make cheddar without a starter of some sort. In Mum's early life, they would take some of yesterday's whey, they'd keep it in a bucket overnight, try to keep it relatively clean, then they'd pour that into the morning's milk that they wanted to get going. So you'd hope that some of the bacteria that made yesterday's acidity would have been growing overnight and would get going again in the morning. You can roll a starter like that for a while and after an indeterminate amount of time the viruses that live on that particular strain of bacteria will breed and the whole thing will eventually die. Then what Mum used to do, you'd go to your neighbour and say, 'Look, I've thrown away today's milk, can I have some of your whey?' So you'd get some of their bacteria which would hopefully be different and you'd get going again. Sometimes if it's a weak type of bacteria and the viruses grow quickly to it, a new starter might only last a week and then that dies as well, and then you have to go further afield to get someone else's whey. There was something really nice and societal about the way this worked, because the more people that come and start using your genetics on their farm, when it dies, if enough people have taken it away, when the rotation comes round, you'll get it back again. So if you've got a good starter it's in everyone's interest to keep it going. So there was this Darwinian evolution happening on farms, because these 300 or so cheesemakers were all doing this. They were gradually breeding better and better starters by swopping and changing them and, because there was raw milk going into them, there was this constant drip feed of new genetics coming from the milk as well. The original genetics were harvested from the farms when all this was going on, when they bred this wonderful mix of bacteria. In the 1950s a guy who was based in Castle Cary went round to all the farms and gathered up all the bacteria and put them in a lab environment to preserve them. And those are the starters we still use today.

There are natural bacterias that are about and are in the milk and they change the way it flavours in the store, they work more slowly. You still have to put the acid bacteria in to start with, but they aren't the whole picture. You've got to have this other wildness to give you the interesting subtleties in the cheddar. Every cheesemaker will have their own pattern of bacteria that they look after in their facility. It's not chance, because I believe the type of bacteria that you have are constantly reaffirmed by the raw milk coming through. What's in your raw milk is dependent on how you look after the cows, what you feed them on, what you bed them down on, all those sorts of things, and it's constantly being topped up by whatever else is happening on the farm.

Turning the cheeses, Manor Farm

The new calf, Manor Farm

Jamie Montgomery

There were a considerable number of cows when Grandpa bought this farm in 1911. It was associated with The Court, so it would not have been the smallest of farms. Everybody had to stop cheesemaking during the War, there was no farmhouse cheese made in the Second World War, all the milk was collected up and sent to prescribed cheese factories. Up until the start of the War there were something like 350 cheesemakers in Somerset. Not many started up again after the War because all the milk was bought after that, and at a good price. I think Grandpa liked the engineering aspects of cheesemaking. It would have been much much easier to stop and just sell the milk, but Grandpa, bless him, he thought, 'Let's do it, let's go back to cheesemaking'.

We breed our own milking cows. We're really doing what Grandpa did and what Mum did, and that's everything. Breeding our own stock was always part of the pattern, it makes perfect sense. It also allows us to select what type of cow we want and we want a cow that is not too big. Over the last 20 years what they call the Holstein has crept into the black and white breed. You can't buy a pure Friesian, they're all Friesian Holstein now, but we can select for body type. We want a strong cow, not too tall. If you were just selling milk you'd want the maximum amount of water you could get out of a cow, but we're not selling milk, we're making cheese. We want the fats and proteins in the milk so we want a slightly smaller cow – she may not give so many litres but she gives the right kind of milk for making cheese. When I was a child our cows were Ayrshire, red and white. The Ayrshire cow has a particularly good fat globule size, great for making hard cheese, and we've been breeding out that gene. So, for the last year, on about half the animals I want to breed from, I've used Ayrshire on them again, I'm breeding it back in.

A lot of cows these days are bedded down on sand and sand drains very well, but I believe that something of the flavour of our unpasteurised milk is coming from the straw. I can't make a big change to what my Grandpa was doing, I've got to place a value on everything that made the cheese as good as my grandfather and Mum were making and that includes having the cows lying on straw. It gives us more challenges but I believe it's worth it. Looking over that gate and seeing those cows lying cosy in a bed of straw in winter, that is significant for me.

Loading the thatching wheat, Courtfield Farm

Courtfield Farm *Milton, Martock*

Tom Dunbar

I left school in 1988 and went straight to New Zealand. I got into a shearing gang for a year, came back and went to Agricultural College, then went back to New Zealand and did more shearing and shepherding. Back here I ended up working on a farm which was growing thatching straw, Brian Oram over in Burrowbridge. I enjoyed it and the thatching idea was sown there really. I got an apprenticeship with Jack Lewis and that was it! Once you've done a four year apprenticeship, you're on the ship aren't you. I always knew I was going to be outside, I was never going to be sat in an office.

Combed wheat is traditional to this area. People often say, 'Surely there's water reed round here', but I've never seen a base coat of water reed, it's always wheat. They were growing wheat and they had to harvest it to get the corn, the straw was a by-product – they'd use it for animal bedding and to thatch the rooves. They also used it for making the cider cheese. Nowadays commercial wheat is grown short, too short for thatching. They don't want the straw. In the old days traditional bread wheats would all have been long-stemmed, a long stem is good for thatching, so it's the traditional bread wheats that we grow for thatching now. It's got to be grown specially for its long stems. There used to be loads of small growers around. There's very few now. I grow my own wheat for thatching. It's been good this year. It's quite critical when you harvest it – what we're looking for is when the nodes are still green and the grain is gone to cottage cheese texture. As you look at it you see a green and orange stripe through the crop, that's when to cut it. You cut it, stook it up, eight sheaves lent up against each other like a tent. That's left for two weeks provided the weather's dry and sunny, or 'three chimes of the church bells' they used to say. Then you bring it in once it's dried through. These days we bale it, it's easier and quicker to handle, and I store it in a heap with sheets over it until we thresh and comb it. Traditionally the individual sheaves were stacked in a rick and processed in the winter months when the labour was about. There were loads of rick-thatchers in the past. Still today some of the old boys you see now, they'll tell you that when they were lads they used to thatch the old ricks. It was a common skill in rural areas, different to house thatchers because it didn't have to be so thick, it only had to last six months to a year.

I love thatching, I couldn't imagine doing anything else. They used to say it was a dying trade, but there are all the listed buildings and some new-build, it's growing in a way. The trouble is not many young fellows seem to want to go into it and, with all the regulations, thatchers aren't taking many apprentices on. I've got an apprentice working with me, I was given the opportunity, so I like to pass it on.

Combing the wheat reed, Holly Farm

Holly Farm *Stoke St Gregory*

Robert Hembrow

I grew up in this house, Holly Farmhouse. My family have been here for five generations. We were a typical Somerset mixed farm with cows, beef cattle, a few sheep, a bit of thatching reed and we grew crops to feed our animals – we grew some brassicas, sometimes some turnips as a cash crop that we could feed to the cows afterwards – but mostly the farm was focussed around the cows. I can remember when I was a small child the cows were milked by hand, in fact my father had to milk them by hand before he went to school when he was a boy. When I was about four years old we got a machine for milking them, albeit into buckets! – and we had a herdsman as well, he stayed here for 38 years. By the time my father died in 1978 there were 45 cows. That was a living. It seems miniscule by today's standards. My parents very rarely went on holiday when I was growing up. We hardly ever went away, money spent was always spent on the farm first, never on anything else. In my younger days we think there were 35 farms just around here that the milk lorry used to call at to collect milk, and now there's only about five farms where he calls – although the number of cows are about the same, or more.

There were more thatched places in the past and more people growing thatching reed, most farms grew a little bit. We always used to grow about six to nine acres, and when I think back, did we ever make hard work of that! We used to pitch the reed by hand when I was young.

When I took over the farm my mother had already stopped milking cows, so I kept beef cattle at first because it was easy to get into and we reared calves, but eventually I could see that this was going to be a huge tie. Then an uncle of mine who was growing thatching reed said this was a good product to be in, and he came and helped me cut my first crop and some friends came and helped with the harvest and we've been doing it ever since. The farm is 63 acres in total and I have it divided it into 30 acres and 33 acres that we alternate between grass and thatching reed, so one year it's 33 acres of reed and the next it's 30 acres. This year we have 33 acres of the wheat reed to harvest.

Loading the combed wheat reed, Holly Farm

Robert Hembrow

Most thatched houses are listed and if you have a wheat reed roof you have to continue with a wheat reed roof, so that's been our saving grace. Somerset and Devon are wheat reed areas, Norfolks's water reed. People growing wheat reed are diminishing all the time because they are mostly of my age and older and getting near retirement.

The threshing machine was built in 1886. The tractor runs it now, but originally it would have been driven by a steam engine. It wouldn't have had the rubber tyres, it would have had iron wheels and it would have been dragged along the road by the steam engine. It's a very clever machine. The lads work up there at the top, feeding the machine with the sheaves one at a time. The wheat passes through drums like enlarged hair curlers, and all the broken bits of straw, the leaves, the dog-legged bits, the short pieces, the bits that won't make thatching reed, they are combed out. The machine sorts it, it does all the work. You end up with the bundles of clean stalks coming out at the bottom – the combed wheat reed ready for the thatcher. And they're tied by the machine. The lads then load them onto the trailer. The by-products are the grain, which goes to a local farmer to feed his cows, the straw bales I sell to horse owners to bed their horses and the chaff goes to a local farm to bed up cubicles because it's friable and goes through the slurry pump. The chaff is blown into the trailer. The chaff is all the little bits around the grains on the ears. Straw's for bedding, the grain's for eating. The machine is a series of sieves and winnowing fans. The broken bits of straw go one way and are baled, the grain goes into the sump and then up through a second winnowing fan and into a grain trailer, and the dust and chaff go off into another trailer – we use everything. We comb it in the winter – it's not a pleasant job, it can be dirty and dusty and cold and really miserable sometimes. It's not hard physical work but it's relentless work because the machine is telling you how fast you've got to go. Thankfully we're under cover, we can keep going if it is raining, but ideally we want a moderate south-westerly breeze to blow the dust away when we're combing and some nice sunny dry weather. It's hidden work. There's a lot of work in a thatched roof that goes on behind the scenes. I'll do it as long as I enjoy it, as long as it's profitable, and as long as I can get enough people to come and help me.

Willowfields *Westonzoyland*

Mike Musgrove

In the 1920s my grandparents rented the house over the road and then bought it. My nan picked broad beans to pay for it, she paid for it over the years. It was a house with a little strip of land on the other side of the road, where we are now, that was all they had. There was already a boiler here because the previous people had done willow sticks. So there's been a withy boiler here for about a hundred years or more.

My grandad was in the First World War, he looked after an officer's horse, then when he came back he used to cut withies. He was a bit of a dealer, and he started buying withies and selling them and he did buff sticks. He rented a couple of fields, but also bought withies standing in the field grown by other people. There were over two thousand acres of willows grown then. The willow auctions were at the Langport Arms. My dad worked on a farm first and then he worked full-time with my grandad on the withies.

Willow growers did quite well in the Second World War. I can remember Dad saying all the willows had to go to the war effort. There were the airborne panniers used to drop supplies, and pigeon baskets, they were big during the war – pigeons took messages, all the tanks had pigeons. Chris Beck's father used to work down here, he used to tie up all the buff bundles. They had quite a few people working here.

They used to supply big basketmaking firms in London. I remember Dad saying that it died out almost overnight when plastics came in – they kept going, but it was a smaller business, they didn't employ so many people.

You always had to strip the willows for the basketmakers. Boiling is a way of stripping the bark, you boil the willow wands and then the bark comes off easily. You boil them for eight hours, it softens them and then you can strip the bark off. In the boiling the tannins come out of the bark and stain the sticks the buff colour. When I was a little boy you used to help do the boiler, jump up and down on the wads of withies to keep them down in the water, peg them down. Then taking them out was a crook and pick job. I did it from when I was about 18 years old until I was about 40. It's hard work, but if you boiled them, left them a day to cool down and pulled them out, that was alright. But if you left them – if you went on cutting and you had a boiler full in there, and you left them for longer – it was twice as hard! It's easier now, I've got a gantry, a cage and a lid, it's much easier. And I've got two new stripping machines so we can strip them in half the time. It depends on the weather how long they take to dry when we tie them up outside. In the summer it may be two or three days, if it's nice and hot.

Jack tying stripped willow to dry, Willowfields

Mike Musgrove

Across the road in front of the house there was a ditch there and when I was a boy they always used to clean out that bit of ditch and put in some big willows. Everybody used to put the willow in ditches in winter then, that was for willow you wanted white. Basketmakers always wanted the willow stripped of the bark. Boiling it is one way, it softens the bark and you can strip it, but that dyes the sticks the brownish colour. If you want it white it has to be stripped in the spring when the sap's rising. So what you did was to cut the willows and keep them growing until the spring. So up through Athelney you used see the ditches and rhines full of the cut willow bundles. It used to be hard work putting them down in the ditch, you used to have to go down in the ditch in your waders, because the water was quite high. You'd do it usually after Christmas. We'd cut them after Christmas, sort them all into sizes, and put the bigger ones – five foot and upwards – in the ditch. You'd stand them in the ditch and tie them up to stop them falling because you could get the wind. Then you'd leave

them till the spring , and at a certain time the sap rises and they start to leaf out. You keep trying them, see if they run, pull out a withy and see if it will strip by hand, see if the bark comes off easily by hand, then it's time to do them – usually May time. When you took them out of the ditch it would be a nightmare, they'd be covered in mud, they were that rooted you couldn't even pull them apart. I do it differently today, I've got them in the yard in a trough, cleaner and easier. These willows that we leave to sprout are all stripped for white willow. People wanted it for cribs and bread baskets in the old days, or for a little strip of white for decoration. We do loads now, about 1,000 wads a year. We like to put a band or plait of white in the coffins, it stands out with the buff, but we also dye some different colours because the white will take the colour.

We sell our willows and we also employ basketmakers making coffins and we make hurdle fencing as well, but we are still selling the willow, that's our main business. Our son Jack is working here now, so he's the fourth generation.

Higher Plot Farm *Aller*

Guy Smith

This farm has been a smallholding for at least 200 years. The room just to the south of us here was the old cider barn. We have a photograph of what they called the 'cider tree', they grew one particularly tall tree to cover the cider barn to keep it cool in summer. The orchard is ancient, it's terraced. It was in the 18th century that apples were really valuable and that's when they would have terraced the orchards we think. We're restoring the orchard and finding unusual, old varieties of apple trees. You can tell a lot about the place from looking at it, working it out. They had cattle, and horses for pulling ploughs and carts, and they would have had other animals, and on one of the old maps, where our vineyard is now, it looks like there was a kind of market garden. Like most of the land round here on the side of the hills overlooking the Levels, it's not really suitable for much else apart from grazing and fruit growing. Talking to local farmers, we knew that Morgan Sweet cider apples did well here and apples ripened early, and that's a good sign that it would be good for grapes. We planted the vineyard in 2008 – Pinot Noir, Pinot Meunier and Chardonnay.

Laura Evans

This is south-west facing, south is ideal, but south-west is good. It's got very good drainage because it's on a limestone slope, and there's fine soil, almost like Burgundian soil, it's limestone and marl – and it's quite well-sheltered, very snug in terms of the landscape. It's a small bowl and where we planted the vineyard it had been a meadow. A gentleman came here some time ago and he explained he was from an Italian family and that his father had been a prisoner of war here. At the top of the hill, just over there, they were working, and they had all said what great slopes they were, how they'd be ideal for a vineyard, he told us.

We had 35 pickers this year, it was a great turnout – lots of people from the villages locally, and friends from as far as Amsterdam. There are pickers who have formed friendships over the years, and it's a really great community thing.

Guy Smith

It was a long cool summer, but we did get the right ripeness, and I think that extra time on the vine in September gives you interesting flavours. That last little bit was key. We could have picked earlier, but they wouldn't have been quite as good, and we held our nerve and picked three weeks later than usual. There's an element of luck though, and one year we may get a frost and not have a crop. The worst moments are frosts late in spring – or hail. It was a lovely crop this year and I took it straight down for pressing that afternoon, on harvest day.

Laura and Guy picking their grapes, Higher Plot Farm

Hecks Cider Farm *Street*

John Hecks

My great-great-grandfather, John Hecks, farmed Lordleaze Farm, a big farm, at Chard – they rented it, but in later years they bought it from Lord Poulett. It was a dairy farm with milking cows, but they'd have had other animals, and chickens. And they made cider. Everyone made cider. In the 1890s there was a bad recession and my grandfather, Thomas Hecks, decided there wasn't a future in the farm so he came up to Street and took on the Street Inn. He thought that would be a better living. He was a tenant, the pub was owned by the Somerton Brewery and he was there for 25 years. In Chard they just made cider for the workers, but my grandfather made cider to sell in the pub in Street, he sold his own cider. Back in those days the pubs used to open at six o'clock in the morning and I remember my father saying the men would be waiting outside – they'd come to the pub to have a drink before they started work at half past six. My grandfather was very knowledgeable about making cider, he brought that knowledge from Chard. As well as running the pub he bought these premises where we are now, he had the press here. Then my father took it on in 1939 – not the pub, just the cider making – and he had a shop. My father made a huge amount of cider during the war, he did well, there was no tax on cider and it was good for cider makers. My father always said so. My grandfather on my mother's side, George Sims, he grew a lot of eating apples in Compton Dundon, and he had a cider orchard, he made cider too. So cider making was in my family on both sides – and on my wife's side too.

Mary Hecks

My family farmed at Wick, just under the Tor. I had to milk five or six cows in the morning then cycle six miles to school. We had working horses, and cows, chickens and always a pig during the war, we were allowed to kill a pig a year in the war. We made cider – every farm made cider. I remember Sunday mornings during the war, there was a crowd that used to start at one end of the lane and work their way round, drinking cider at each farm. We were the last farm they came to, so our Sunday lunch didn't used to be until about three o'clock! We didn't make cider commercially, no money changed hands. You gave it away. Tramps used to come up. The workhouse was in Wells and I remember there were two old chaps, they'd come twice a year. They'd walk from Wells, and Mum used to give them a bread and cheese lunch and they'd have a couple of pints of cider, and then she'd give them a piece of cake to take on with them and they'd walk back to Wells to the workhouse. Cider's been in both our families. Now it's our sons, Andrew and Chris, who run the business, they're fifth generation cider makers.

Andrew Hecks in the Glastonbury orchard, blossom time

Charlton Orchards *Creech St Michael*

Robin Small

I went into fruit growing after National Service in the late 1950s and we came to Somerset to find work. There was a fruit grower at Kingston St Mary who was desperate for someone to come and help him prune the orchard and get rid of the apples, and there was another fruit grower at Creech – they both had orchards to be pruned and sheds full of apples. Within a week I was down here and my wife, June, followed at the end of term because she got a job teaching in the village school.

Mr Greenshields was the name of the fruit grower at Creech and he was originally one of the farmers during the Second World War that was asked to take on failing farms to grow fruit and vegetables for Britain. If farmers were failing and not producing enough food, then the Government put somebody in to do it and he was one of those who came down and he ran the farm. Then after the war there was no need for the Farming for Britain and he bought the farm, Charlton Farm. It was a dairy farm. There was no orchard then, but he was getting on, so in 1947 he

decided he would plant a little orchard on four acres. One family could run the orchard quite well – they couldn't do it now and make a living, but they could then. He planted that orchard in 1947 and later sold the rest of the farm on.

When Mr Greenshields established the orchard he planted something like 12 or 13 varieties plus some damsons as a wind break and a few pears. We've still got some of the original old varieties of apples in the orchard – Worcester Pearmain, Lord Lambourne, Kidds Orange, Cox's Orange Pippin, Egremont Russet, Adams Pearmain, Orleans Reinette and Ashmead's Kernel.

There were acres of orchards fifty years ago, apples for eating and cider orchards. When I was first here I could have sat here and named 30 apple growers all around, locally or fairly local, that's apples for eating. By the end of the 70s and into the 80s it became very difficult to live on a small acreage, so a lot of those small farmers went out. They couldn't see a prospect. You see you could make a living on four acres before the middle of the 1970s and the supermarket era.

Duncan Small

Historically, years ago, there was a good market for apples in Wales. The very traditional Somerset apple, Morgan Sweet, was sent to South Wales, because it went very well with Caerphilly cheese and the miners used to take it down the mines to eat with their cheese. There was a ferry link between Minehead and Barry and lots of Morgan Sweets were exported to South Wales.

It's good pasture land here in Somerset and when standard trees used to be tall you could run stock underneath, so you got a double crop – cattle or sheep underneath, and apples above. That was good for mixed farms, when there were so many mixed farms with a mix of crops and animals, which was what most Somerset farms were. We are not a mixed farm now as we might have been in the past, we are a fruit farm, and we have to maximise what we get off our trees, so they're much closer together, much smaller. They've got to be closer to the ground so they're easier to pick and that means you can't run stock underneath them.

We often have mothers picking with their children, families too – last year we had three generations of one family picking. The crab apple trees are here for pollination, they are bitter to eat, too bitter – they are a decorative tree really. They look really beautiful when they are in fruit, but we grow them for their fantastic amount of pollen, it brings in the insects. Bees are really good pollinators but there are lots of other insects – hoverflies and other little flies. Our hedgerows tend to be rather untouched, so there will be a build-up of insects, then if bees are thin on the ground there are plenty of others. Chris Harries brings his hives into the orchards, but there are also colonies of wild bees here and bumble bees.

Sally Bail

The season starts with pruning the trees. This is finished by March or April – it's all by hand. Then it's sowing seeds, planting and pricking out plants, and there are the daffodils we grow, then the soft fruits come in by June or July, then it's picking apples and pears. We finish picking apples and pears normally by the middle of October and then all the pickers go away and we're back to our core staff. Then we work through our cold stores, bringing the fruit out, getting it out to local markets, farm shops and so on, and that goes on until, well, depending how big the crop is, that will go on until the end of February. We can tell the potential for the coming season quite early. Apples like a good mix of average British weather, so the sort of weather that makes holidaymakers moan actually doesn't do apples any harm at all.

Picking pears , Charlton Orchards

Burrow Hill Cider *Kingsbury Episcopi*

Julian Temperley

My father was brought up in the village here. One side of our family are the Bradfords. Great-great-grandfather used to bring coal from South Wales up the River Parrett and unload it at Thorney down the road and distribute it. They went on to become the builders' merchants. The agricultural part of the Bradfords' empire was growing basketmaking willows on the Levels here. So we are part of the Somerset story. My father was a nuclear physicist and I grew up in Cambridge and Hampshire, but our links to Somerset have always been strong. My father still lives down the road, aged 102, in the house that was built by his great-grandfather, Job Bradford.

Somerset is a land of small farms, a land of working countryside. This was a small farm, one of the most respected cider farms in the area. It was owned by a family called Ducks – two sisters and a brother. They were quite old and decided to retire. In their time they had cows, grew corn, had a few sheep. We still keep sheep, but the cider has expanded and taken over.

If a cider apple has 'Jersey' in the name it means it originated in South Somerset – the island of Jersey has nothing to do with it. 'Jaisey' was a South Somerset dialect word for cider apple. When people came to write it down they translated it as 'Jersey' – there's Harry Masters Jersey, Stembridge Jersey, Coate Jersey and others. These apples originated round here. Dabinett is a Kingsbury variety, it was originally found in about 1937 by a man called Mr Dabinett in a hedge in Mid Lambrook, about a mile from here. If you go to Drayton Church you can see Dabinett graves. It is the most important single variety of cider apple, but the art and craft of making cider in Somerset is in the blending of apples. You have sweet and sharp apples: sharp apples – high in acid and low in tannin, bitter sharp apples – high in tannin and high in acid, and bittersweet apples – low acid and high tannin. In the same way as Champagne is made in France by blending three varieties of grapes, cider is a blend of varieties of apples. Traditionally a farm orchard would have had cider apples, a few eating apples and some cooking apples (nice sharp apples, like Bramley or Newton Wonder, for the farmer's wife to make a pie) and they were all blended together. We grow on this farm now 40 varieties of apples and we blend them to make our artisan cider – no concentrates, no enzymes.

Once you finish cider making, you do the drains and other things on the farm that need doing, then the pruning starts about 1st February and goes on until the beginning of May. Pruning we never finish. We do what we need to do and we prioritise. By the time the spring starts coming there are other things to do on the farm – there's a time when the sap is coming up and it's time to stop. Cider trees are relatively tolerant but some varieties need serious attention, especially when they are young.

Carl with the blower, Over Stratton orchard

Julian Temperley

The orchard at Over Stratton is our biggest orchard – 73 acres, 20 different varieties of apples. In the picture, that's a patch of Yarlington Mill apples, named after the village of Yarlington, about twenty miles from here. It's a bittersweet apple – almost all that orchard are bittersweet apples. The orchard was planted in the 1950s by the Showering family, of Babycham fame. We were lucky enough to buy it about 30 years ago – and save it really – because in those days people didn't appreciate orchards. It's probably the biggest standard orchard in Europe. If you stand in the middle you can't see out – 360 degrees all round and you can only see orchards into the distance. When we come to harvest it's quite daunting, because it will take three of four guys a solid month working with quite cunning machines. This year we had a huge crop.

We often need to shake the trees to loosen the last apples. Then, when the apples are all on the ground, we blow the leaves off, depending how much leaf is down. We have a tractor with a fan on the back, so, when the harvester comes on behind, most of the leaves have been blown away. You need clean apples to press and we harvest very late, when the starch in the apple has all turned to sugar. The apples are on the ground, but if there's a huge pile of leaves with them, that causes a bit of a problem. It's a Massey Ferguson 65 which powers the blower – it's a truly joyous tractor with a nice roar, it's not very warm, but it's better than sitting in an enclosed, more modern tractor which can often sound like a giant sewing machine!

Early varieties we harvest in October and then we go on harvesting right up to Christmas. In the old days they sometimes picked up apples early and then put them in a heap in the orchard. Then they would go back after Christmas and shovel them up into a trailer and take them to the press. Getting apples ripe requires a long season and then you need to get apples pressed before they go rotten. We want apples to fall into the grass, they're protected from the frost in the grass. This year we had a very good year – the weather wasn't conducive to rotting, so the apples were perfect throughout the season. In the end we finished picking up apples six hours before we shut down for Christmas.

We want to do justice to the traditions of apple orchards, so we need to be pure juice cider in the same way wine is made, and that's the same with our brandy, it's distilled from the pure juice cider. There is a huge wish nowadays for people to have good local products. We see our future in the cider brandy (the distilling's a really important part of the business now), and in the up-market cider we supply to top restaurants, as well as the farm cider that we continue to sell in all sorts of containers from the farm.

The Lockyer family picking cider apples

Woodpecker Lodge Farm *Bere Aller*

Jimmy Lockyer

I have lived here on the farm for 70 years. The earliest thing I can remember is milking cows by hand, my mother and father used to milk about 20 cows by hand and I used to go out and sit on the stool and help them milk the cows, that was my earliest memory. We kept cows and a few sheep, and my father ran a boar service. He used to keep a boar for other people to bring their sows to go the boar and he did it for years and years and years. All the people from Othery and Middlezoy and High Ham used to bring their sows down here. I remember when it was about ten shillings a time, and the last one was about 25 shillings. Bill Hodge used to bring his sow down here on a horse and cart.

Mary Lockyer

My great-grandfather made cider and as children we used to have to go and help pick the apples. We were expected to help my parents and grandparents and uncles on the farm – moving cows, moving sheep, turning the handle on the sheep-shearing machine, everything was done by hand. I remember the cider making when I was very young. It was a communal thing, where all the village people used to come in and help. Everyone would be picking and then they'd be sitting there telling yarns in the sheds when the apples were being pressed. Whereas today we'll make a cider cheese and it will be done and finished and we'll get on with the next one, they used to make a cider cheese perhaps once a week, it wasn't made in big quantities. Going back 50 years you made it for yourselves and your neighbours, it wasn't commercial. Then all the apple pomace used to be fed to the pigs – the pomace is what's left when the juice is pressed out – so nothing was wasted. There were always pigs and sheep in the orchards, and cows and calves. When we pick the apples now all the family come and help. I've been picking apples since I was knee-high and our grandchildren started when they were young too.

The Lockyer family pressing apples for cider

Jimmy Lockyer

Mary's family always made cider, they'd sit down with a glass of cider with their bread and cheese for their supper, that was the only cider they would drink, they wouldn't touch it during the day. I used to supply them with some apples because there were cider apples here on the farm and then in 1983 we moved their cider press here and we all made the cider here. It was always a communal thing and fun. It was rough cider, it was what everyone used to make. The rough cider drinkers have disappeared really, they were characters. One chap who used to work for my neighbour up here, they said he used to go off to work all day with a packet of fags and a bottle of cider, that's all he would have. Years ago there wasn't much entertainment and there weren't so many distractions, so they used to enjoy sitting in the cider shed. They'd been working all day, they'd bring out a bit of bread and cheese and they'd sit there and have a chat, which is sadly missing today. We used to make the cider cheese with straw and there was an art to it, making sure the cheese didn't fall over – because if you'd been building it up with straw, they had a nasty knack of falling over and you sometimes wondered how it stood there and all that was holding it together was the straw. We only use the cloth now because it's cleaner. Mother-in-law used to say, 'Don't use fusty straw or you won't be able to drink the cider, make sure you get some nice clean straw'. But you wouldn't make the cider until October/November-time and the straw had been combine-harvested in August/September, so they'd already had it for a month or so, plus it was in the shed. She'd say, 'Go and pick me out a nice clean bale of straw', but you never knew what had been on the straw – you just didn't know!

Mary Lockyer

They never used to waste anything. I remember my grand-father making the cider cheese in the press with the straw, it used to be so tall, sitting there for three or four days just drip, drip, drip, all the apple juice dripping through. Then he used to take it all off and just have the hay knife and shear it all the way around and pack it back on the top so it was like a thatched house, and then press it down again for another two or three days – just to get an extra jugful.

West Croft Cider Farm *Brent Knoll*

John Harris

My grandfather bought this farm in 1918, but it was in the family before that. It was a typical Somerset mixed farm with a few milking cows, hens and pigs. We've got a cheese room in the house, so they would have made cheese. They had a few sheep to follow on from the cows, and they made hay, and there was a cider orchard. Cider making and cider orchards were a big part of the rural set-up here. The original cider house was here when my grandfather bought the farm. Just about every farm around here made a drop of cider. The tradition's carried on in some places, in other places it's died out, mostly in the 1970s. We were mainly dairy when I was a child. We had 70 cows and all the followers on 200 acres. There were 11 dairy farms around here, now there are two. We were the first dairy farm to sell our cows, in about 1986. I left for some years and worked as a photographer. I'd planted orchards before I left and when I came back in 1992 I resurrected the cider making. A hundred years ago there were 30 acres of cider orchards on the west-facing slopes of Brent Knoll, all owned by different people – it was covered in cider orchards. That's gone, but we've still got three acres up there. It's brilliant apple growing country because of the aspect, because you get a vintner's quality to the cider apples, like wine – you've got the west-facing slope, and the Severn Estuary reflecting all the light back up into the apples. I've got about 1000 apple trees on about eight acres altogether.

The wassailing started about 20 years ago, there weren't many doing it then. Rob Wilson pressed me and the first one was here with about eight of us. We stood round this old tree, put a ring of candles around the trunk, tipped cider round the roots and a bit of toast, sang a few songs and then proceeded into the evening with the cider. The next year we got the Morris Men involved and a few more people turned up and then the Langport Mummers joined in. Wassailing is something that was forgotten about as cider went out of fashion. Grants were given to grub-up orchards, a lot of orchards were taken out.

Our wassail has evolved. We have the wassailing song and the 'hatfulls and capfulls' shout – a sort of toast to the tree. You're getting into country traditions – mummers are a good old country tradition, and we have flaming torches, the candlelit procession, the wassailing queen carried in, and shotguns. It's traditional, it's English, it's a bit off-the-wall! The ceremony includes it all – there's a lot of noise, shouting and banging saucepans, and singing. There are reasons for these things that you might not expect. The hitting of the tree in the middle of winter can dislodge harmful insects, noise can have an effect on things, perhaps it's good husbandry. These ceremonies keep the knowledge going, which is good.

Directory of Somerset farms

Burrow Hill Cider, Pass Vale Farm *Kingsbury Episcopi* (Somerset Cider Brandy Company) *pages 62–65*

The farm was a traditional small mixed farm when Julian Temperley bought it in 1968. The farm has been making cider for over 150 years and distilling cider into Somerset Cider Brandy since 1989. It was the first cider farm to have a distilling license in recent history, although references to distilling cider can be found in old books on cider making. The farm is situated at the foot of Burrow Hill with its one tree, a local landmark. The cider house on the farm is open six days a week, selling traditional draught cider, sparkling cider, cider brandy and other local produce. The blue Burrow Hill Cider Bus is well-known at the Glastonbury Festival. Julian and his wife, Diana, also keep sheep on the farm. *www.ciderbrandy.co.uk*

Butleigh Road Farm *Glastonbury* *pp. 14–19*

Les Davies worked as a cowman in Street when he left school in 1952, aged 15. He has been a dairy farmer in Glastonbury for over 50 years. His son, Colin, has worked with him for 40 years. Colin's son, Thomas, joined them when he left school in 2006, and Colin's step-grandson, Cory, also works with them. The four generations farm together. They went organic in 2000 and sell their organic milk in bulk. They rent land and own some and make their own hay and silage for the cows.

Butterwell Farm *Pitney* *pp. 10–13*

Pete Cox is the fourth generation of his family farming Butterwell Farm. His great-grandfather bought it in 1923 and his grandparents and parents continued running it as a traditional small self-sufficient mixed farm. In more recent years Pete focussed on his small dairy herd and followers. He also took on other contracting work. The drawings, paintings and interviews were made in 2015–16. Pete stopped milking in the summer of 2016 and is now rearing calves. He sold most of his cows to Luke Timewell, who was starting up (*see* Southend Farm).

Charlton Orchards *Creech St Michael* *pp. 58–61*

There was a traditional dairy farm here until about 1950 when it was sold. Part of the land was retained as orchards and Charlton Orchards has been growing traditional varieties of fruit for over 60 years, a partnership between the Small and Freudenberg families. Duncan Small and his partner, Sally Bail, grow apples, pears, plums, soft fruit, pumpkins and daffodils. They also produce a range of single variety apple juices and grow bare-root fruit trees, bushes and kitchen garden plants. They sell their produce on the farm and at local markets.
www.charltonorchards.com

Courtfield Farm *Milton, Martock* *p. 45*

Tom Dunbar is a professional Master Thatcher and Courtfield Farm is a thriving smallholding. Tom grows his own wheat for thatching and processes it in the field with fellow Master Thatcher, Nigel Bunce, and their vintage thrashing (combing) machine. Plants are grown by Tom's partner, Amanda, a plantswoman, gardener and garden designer, and she and Tom also keep sheep and chickens. Tom also makes traditional cider from their orchard, using an old cider press rescued from a bonfire in Normandy.
www.tomdunbarthatcher.co.uk

Cracknell's Farm *Langport* *p. 27*

Tony Cracknell came from a farming family and he and his wife, Eileen, started the farm from scratch in 1954.

They have been rearing free-range additive-free poultry for over half a century and their son, Jeff, and his family, now run the farm. The birds come as day-old chicks and remain on the farm throughout their lives. Their heating comes from renewable energy (woodchips). There are approximately 2,000 chickens roaming nine acres of pasture, and about 200 ducks. They also rear geese for Christmas and New Year and keep sheep (100 breeding ewes). Poultry is processed on the farm and sold by local butchers, farm shops and from the door.
www.cracknellsfarm.com

Jeff with the new chicks, Cracknell's Farm

Glebe Farm *Pitney* *pp.20–25*

Edwin Walrond was a tenant farmer in the 19th century and then bought the farm. David Walrond, his grandson, took it on in the 1980s. His son and daughter-in-law, Rob and Lizzie, now run it as an organic farm with its own farm shop. They grow vegetables and rear cattle, sheep, pigs and hens. Pitney Farm Shop sells their own meat, home-made sausages, free-range eggs and home-grown vegetables, also other local produce (including the produce of several farmers featured in this book). The Walronds also open their farm for educational and other events. A café serving locally grown food opens on the farm in the summer 2017. *www.pitneyfarmshop.co.uk*

Hecks Cider Farm *Street* *p.56*

The Hecks family has been making traditional farmhouse cider for six generations. Thomas Hecks began making cider on the present site in the late 1890s. Today his great-grandsons, Chris and Andrew Hecks, make traditional ciders which are fermented in wood barrels and sold bottled and draught. They also make perry and apple juice from their own fruit. Their farm shop also sells their honey, locally grown vegetables, fruit, local cheeses and other produce. *www.heckscider.co.uk*

Rob Walrond with the lambs and their mother

Higher Plot Farm *Aller*   *p.55*

Higher Plot Farm was a traditional family smallholding until the 1990s. Guy Smith and Laura Evans bought it in 2007 after a four-year search for a good site to plant a vineyard. Guy also works as a wine trader and Laura works in film editing. Their sparkling wine has won many awards. They also make cider and have plans to make gin. The year referred to in the text on page 55 is 2015, which is when the interview was recorded and the drawings and paintings of the grape harvest made.

www.smithandevans.co.uk
www.somersetcidercompany.co.uk

Holly Farm *Stoke St Gregory*   *pp.46–49*

Robert Hembrow took over the family farm in 1985. It was a traditional Somerset farm, with small dairy herd and crops grown for bedding and fodder, also a small amount of wheat reed for thatching. Milking stopped in the early 1980s. Robert and his wife converted farm buildings for holiday lets and Robert has specialised in growing and processing wheat reed. His wheat threshing machine dates from 1886 and was once powered by steam.

Overton Farm *Babcary*   *p.35*
(Hurdlebrook)

George Paull was a first generation tenant dairy farmer and cattle dealer in the 1940s and bought Overton Farm in the early 1960s. His son Ken purchased the neighbouring Olive Farm. Now Dave Paull, third generation, with Rosie Sage, and their daughters Jenny and Chloe, run the combined farms as one unit, with 200 Guernsey cows plus followers. They sell their yoghurt, crème fraiche and unpastuerised milk and cream through local outlets, farmers' markets and from the farm. Their raw Guernsey milk is also made into cheese by a local cheesemaker.
www.hurdlebrook.co.uk

Manor Farm *North Cadbury*   *pp.40–43*

Sir Archibald Langman bought Manor Farm in 1911. He was one of very few farmers who re-started cheese-making when it was permitted again after the Second World War. The cheesemaking was continued by his daughter, Elizabeth Montgomery, and today by her son, Jamie. The award-winning Montgomery Cheddar is made from unpasteurised milk from their own cows. Jamie also makes a raclette cheese from their Jersey herd (named Ogleshield after the Bronze Age shield excavated at South Cadbury). The cheeses are sold in North Cadbury Village Store and shops and delicatessens across the country. Jamie's brother, Archie, runs the arable side of the farm. *www.montgomerycheese.co.uk*

School Farm *Muchelney* *pp.30–33*

School Farm is a traditional small mixed farm run by Graham and Helen Walker. Graham's great-grandfather, Charles Brister, came as a tenant farmer in the 1890s and purchased it in the 1920s when the landlord needed to raise funds to pay death duties. It was a dairy farm until the 1960s. It comprises 47 acres of mainly moorland which often floods in winter. The Walkers rear cattle, Oxford Sandy and Black pigs, and sheep. They also grow vegetables. They run a farm shop which sells their home-made pies, meat and other produce, also cream teas in the summer. *www.schoolfarmmuchelney.co.uk*

Southend Farm *High Ham* *p.36*

When Luke Timewell left school in 2008 he was employed as a farmworker in Henley, near High Ham. He and his partner, Abbie Jarvis, began building up a herd of milking cows in 2015, buying them from Pete Cox, who was giving up (*see* Butterwell Farm). By January 2017 they were milk-ing 16, with calves coming on, and the herd increasing. They rent the farm buildings, which are now known as Southend Farm. They also rent the land. They make their own hay and silage, take on agricultural contracting work and sell their milk in bulk.

Phil picking grapes, Higher Plot Farm

Sunnyside Farm *North Wootton*   *p.29*
(North Wootton Organic Dairy)

North Wootton overlooks the Somerset Levels on the slopes
of the South Mendip hills. The Bartlett family has been
farming here since the 1960s. In 1999 James and Dave Bartlett took over the running of the farm. They make artisan,
hand-made cheese from the milk from their sheep and Jersey
cows, and yoghurt from the ewes' milk, which they sell at
farmers' markets and local shops. They also rear cattle.
www.woottondairy.com

Westcombe Dairy, Lower Westcombe Farm *Evercreech*   *p.39*

Unpasteurised cheddar was made at Westcombe by Mr
and Mrs Brickell in the early 1900s and, before that, by
Edith Cannon, a renowned cheesemaker. In the 1960s
Richard Calver joined the family business at Westcombe
Dairy, where they were making block cheddar at the time.
In the 1990s the farm returned to making traditional farmhouse cheddar, which has been developed by Richard's
son, Tom, a trained chef, who joined the business in 2003.
They make award-winning cheddar, caerphilly and ricotta
from the unpasteurised milk from their cows. They have
recently completed building a 'cave' for maturing their
cheese. Their cheeses are available from the farm, also shops
and delicatessens nationwide.
www.westcombedairy.com

Ivor Hancock, basketmaker

West Croft Cider Farm *Brent Knoll*   *p.70*

The farm was a traditional dairy farm until the 1980s and has been in the Harris family for over 100 years. Historically cider was made here for the workers, as it was on most Somerset farms. John Harris now specialises in growing apples for his award-winning cider which he sells on the farm and through other outlets. He also sells cider vinegar. The annual West Croft Cider Wassail in January is a large event, involving the traditional Wassail ceremony with gunshot, mummers play, dancers, live band and other entertainments.
E *johnharris554@gmail.com*

Willowfields *Westonzoyland*   *p.50–53*

Mike Musgrove's grandfather cut willow sticks for furniture in the 1920s. Mike's father cultivated his own willow and Mike joined the family business when he left school. The acreage increased over the years and the willow farm is now run by Mike, his wife Ellen, and son Jack. The Musgrove family and their employees supply buff, white and coloured willow to basketmakers and sculptors, and willow charcoal for drawing. They also make willow coffins, hurdles and baskets, and run courses.
www.musgrovewillows.co.uk

Woodpecker Lodge Farm *Bere Aller* *   *pp.66–69*

Jimmy Lockyer grew up on the farm adjacent to Woodpecker Lodge. He and his family make cider using a traditional cider press. They put on a Wassail in January. Their Gold Rush cider and bottled sparkling cider are made from local apples, many grown in their own orchards. Cider can be sampled and purchased in their 'Cider Shack', which also sells their apple juice, cider vinegar and other local produce. Jimmy also rears cattle.
www.berecidercompany.com

* Bere is also known as Beer

The paintings and drawings

*All works are oil on paper or board except those marked with an * which are charcoal, pastel or pencil. Measurements are in centimeters.*

cover	Carl with the blower, Burrow Hill Cider, Over Stratton	25 × 32
half title	Cider apples for pressing	37 × 30
frontispiece	Baling grass for silage, Butleigh Road Farm	26 × 25
imprints page	Broadcasting grass seed with the fiddle*	41 × 34
back cover	Jeff Cracknell and the Christmas geese	14 × 14
6	Preparatory sketch for charcoal drawing on p.66	
7	Preparatory sketch for charcoal drawing on p. 34	
9	The Saddleback sow and piglets, Glebe Farm	14 × 21
10	Milking time, Butterwell Farm	13 × 14
13	Pete milking, Butterwell Farm	13 × 14
15	Les and Colin in the yard, Butleigh Road Farm*	66 × 102
16	Thomas in the barn, Butleigh Road Farm	34 × 39
18	Baling grass for silage, Butleigh Road Farm	26 × 25
21	Rob feeding the sow and piglets, Glebe Farm	21 × 26
23	Running the flock from the moor up to Glebe Farm	33 × 37
24	The hen house, Glebe Farm	34 × 46
26	Jeff Cracknell and the Christmas geese	14 × 14
28	James milks the ewes, Sunnyside Farm	47 × 33
31	Graham on the moor, November	27 × 36
32	Graham scraping the yard, January	17 × 20
34	David brings in the cows, Overton Farm*	57 × 46
37	Luke and the milking bail, Southend Farm	30 × 40
38	Rob cheddaring the curd, Westcombe Dairy	18 × 20
41	Turning the cheeses, Manor Farm	36 × 39
42	The new calf, Manor Farm*	45 × 55

The voices

The words of the farmers are taken from informal interviews recorded and transcribed by Kate Lynch during 2015–17. Extracts were selected to accompany her paintings and drawings, and the text was approved by the farmers, with occasional edits. There is one exception: the words of James Bartlett (page 29) were taken from an interview made by Ann Heeley in 2008 for the Somerset Heritage Centre. James updated the text for this book.

Many other farmers have been interviewed by Ann Heeley MBE, Friends of the Somerset Rural Life Museum. The Somerset Voices archive is managed by the South West Heritage Trust and can be accessed at the Somerset Heritage Centre. Somerset Voices includes over 800 fully transcribed interviews. Details of the recordings can be found on the Somerset Archives and Local Studies Online Catalogue, *www.somerset-cat.swheritage.org.uk*. Listen to recordings at the Somerset Heritage Centre by booking an appointment.

SOMERSET HERITAGE CENTRE
Brunel Way
Langford Mead
Norton Fitzwarren   T   01823 278805
Taunton TA2 6SF   W   swheritage.org.uk

Tom Dunbar thatching

Acknowledgements

My love affair with the Somerset Levels began when we arrived here in 1999. We moved only twenty miles further west in Somerset, but here on the Levels was an unfamiliar landscape, with different crops, smaller fields, ditches and rhines – and sometimes floods. There were peat diggers, willow growers, cider makers and many farmers with small mixed farms. They were often following in the footsteps of their grandparents and great-grandparents – rooted in a landscape they knew like the back of their hand. And so a journey began into this unfamiliar territory as I took my sketchbook into sheds, barns, fields and orchards and listened to stories.

Although greatly reduced in number, there are very many working farms in Somerset. This book features a small selection and is the result of a two-year collaboration with these farmers and their families. I would like to thank them for their generous welcome, for describing their seasonal work, and for sharing their memories of a time when the cow had as much right to the road as the car.

Thanks also to the following people for their support and contributions: Tom Mayberry, Chief Executive at South West Heritage Trust, also Sam Astill and Lawrence Bostock; The Elmgrant Trust, The Lark Trust, Friends of the Somerset Rural Life Museum and other benefactors; Ann and David Heeley; Tracey Baker and Sue Young; Alastair Goolden; Lyn Davies; Richard Sainsbury at Delmar Studio; Steve Rose and Hamptons; and family, friends and patrons who have given encouragement along the way.

KATE LYNCH

Kate has spent nearly 40 years as a painter, community artist and art teacher. This is her fourth book. Her previous books are: *Willow* (2003), *Sheep, from Lamb to Loom* (2009) and *The Beekeeper and the Bee* (2012). Kate is married to the landscape artist, James Lynch, and they live in High Ham. *www.katelynch.co.uk*

Afterword

David Walrond, Glebe Farm *Pitney*

We were always busy, one season ran into another. When you got to spring you ploughed the ground, got your corn in, then you put your mangolds in, then once they were up you'd go through them with the horse-hoe and cut the weeds out. You cut as close to the drills as you could, so then when the horse-hoe had been through you'd single them out, or we'd say we were going 'striking them out', that was the same as singling. Then you'd go in with the hand-hoe and weed round the individual plants. Then that would run straight on into haymaking and that would run on into harvest. So there was not a lot of spare time. And then there were the animals all the time. They would come in for the winter. Yes, a lot of work. And milking twice a day every day. I often think about the hand milking – I mean sometimes it would be absolutely pouring with rain and you'd be sat there in the rain milking on your stool ….

Chloe brings the cows in, Butterwell Farm